Ultimate
Lit'l Ukulele Chords, plus

by Kahuna Uke
aka Ron Middlebrook

The last ukulele chord book you'll ever need.
You'll say mahalo later!

ISBN 978-1-57424-256-0
SAN 683-8022

Cover by James Creative Group

In C Tuning
How To Begin, Complete
Chord Charts, Principal
Chords in Major & Minor
Keys, Chord Positions,
Modulations, Note Study
& Scales on all Strings.

CENTERSTREAM®

Most of this lit'l chord book has been scanned from several of the earliest ukulele books we could find. One was from 1916. Therefore, some of the scans might not be as sharp as they could be.

Contents:

The **Ukulele**

The **Ukulele-Banjo**

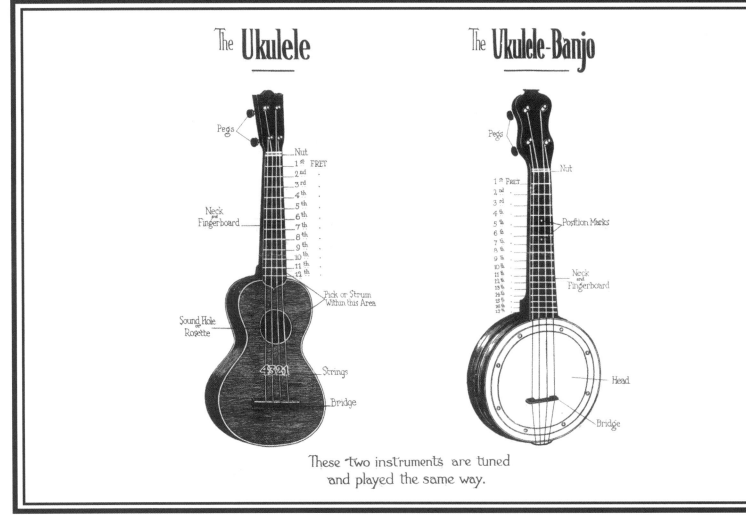

The Ukulele labels:
Pegs
Nut
1st FRET
2nd
3rd
4th
5th
6th
7th
8th
9th
10th
11th
12th
Neck and Fingerboard
Pick or Strum Within this Area
Sound Hole or Rosette
4 3 2 1
Strings
Bridge

The Ukulele-Banjo labels:
Pegs
Nut
1st FRET
2nd
3rd
4th
5th
6th
7th
8th
9th
10th
11th
12th
13th
14th
15th
16th
17th
Position Marks
Neck and Fingerboard
Head
Bridge

These two instruments are tuned
and played the same way.

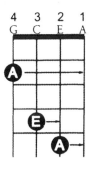

Relative Tuning

Whenever a pitch pipe, piano or another tuned ukulele is not available to you for tuning, the relative tuning method can be used. This method will allow the uke to be in tune with itself, but not necessarily in tune with any other instrument.

1. Turn the tuning peg of the 1st string (A) until it is fairly tight and produces a high tone.
2. Press the 5th fret of the 2nd string (E) and tune to equal the pitch of the 1st string (A).
3. Press the 4th fret of the 3rd string (C) and tune to equal the pitch of the 2nd string (E).
4. Press the 2nd fret of the 4th string (G) and tune to equal the pitch of the 1st string (A).

Ukulele Fingerboard

If you see the sharp symbol #, it means to *raise* the pitch one fret higher. The flat symbol b means to *lower* the pitch one fret back.

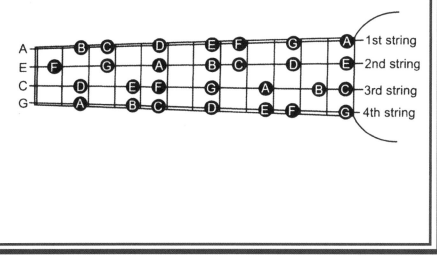

How to begin:

Correct playing position

The middle of the fight forearm should press the back of the ukulele to the body, firmly enough to prevent its slipping (or you can use a handy Centerstream Ukulele strap) so it may be played in either a sitting or standing position.

The left arm should be extended forward. Holding the neck of the ukulele between the thumb and joint of the first finger, with the tip of the thumb resting approximately at the side of the first fret.

Pick Style Playing:

Using the pick

Position of the left or fretting hand and fingers:

Study these pictures carefully; notice the position of the thumb, resting at the side of the neck near the first fret. The finger is curved in position to contact the strings, and the palm is held away from the neck.

The front view shows the fingers in place for chording. Notice that only the fingertips are used and placed behind the frets not on them

The Common Stroke

There are several different strokes that are effective in various styles of music. For the present we give only the "Common" stroke that is the basis of all the others and must be thoroughly mastered before any of the more complicated are attempted.

The Common Stroke is made by dragging the first finger of the right hand lightly down and up across all the strings at the upper edge of the sound hole. Try to relax the hand at all times, the stroke being made entirely with the wrist which must be perfectly free in its motion. Keep the wrist high.
Make the down stroke squarely on the nail of the first finger, and the up stroke with the ball of fleshy part.

COMPLETE CHORD CHART FOR UKULELE

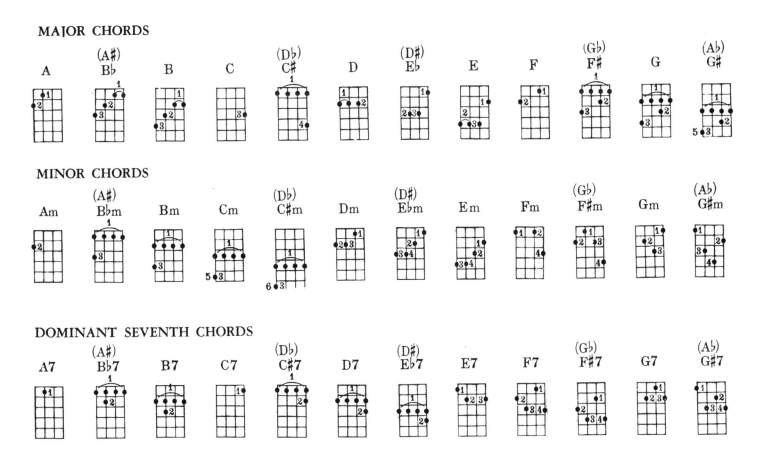

COMPLETE CHORD CHART FOR UKULELE

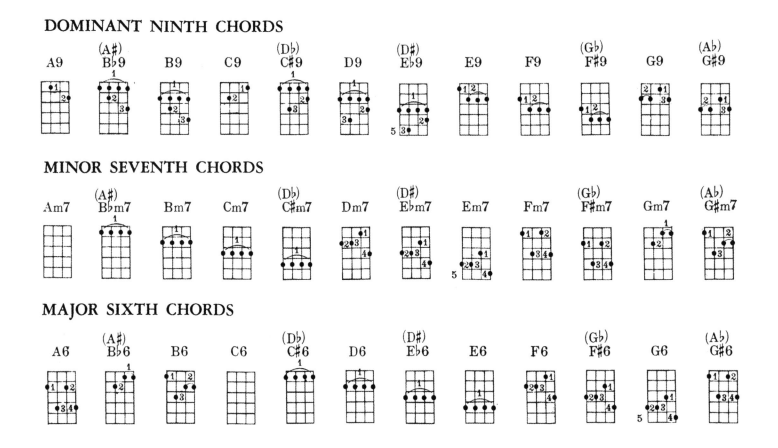

DOMINANT NINTH CHORDS

MINOR SEVENTH CHORDS

MAJOR SIXTH CHORDS

COMPLETE CHORD CHART FOR UKULELE

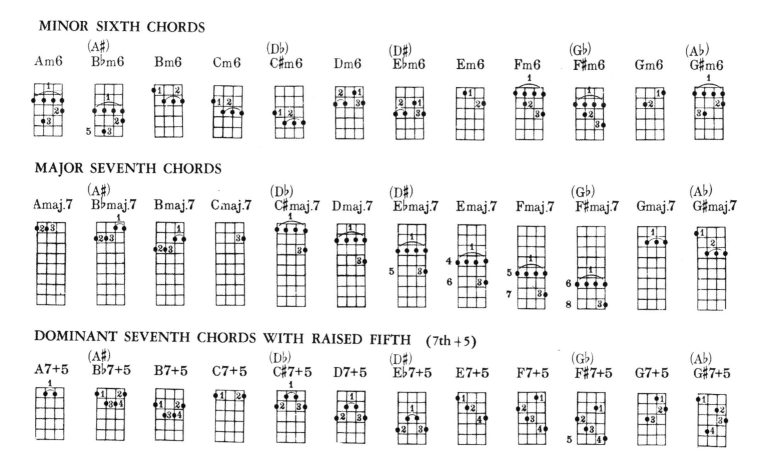

MINOR SIXTH CHORDS

Am6   (A#) B♭m6   Bm6   Cm6   (D♭) C#m6   Dm6   (D#) E♭m6   Em6   Fm6   (G♭) F#m6   Gm6   (A♭) G#m6

MAJOR SEVENTH CHORDS

Amaj.7   (A#) B♭maj.7   Bmaj.7   Cmaj.7   (D♭) C#maj.7   Dmaj.7   (D#) E♭maj.7   Emaj.7   Fmaj.7   (G♭) F#maj.7   Gmaj.7   (A♭) G#maj.7

DOMINANT SEVENTH CHORDS WITH RAISED FIFTH   (7th + 5)

A7+5   (A#) B♭7+5   B7+5   C7+5   (D♭) C#7+5   D7+5   (D#) E♭7+5   E7+5   F7+5   (G♭) F#7+5   G7+5   (A♭) G#7+5

9

COMPLETE CHORD CHART FOR UKULELE

DOMINANT SEVENTH CHORDS WITH LOWERED FIFTH (7th—5)

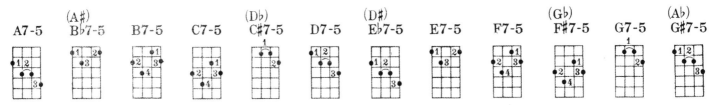

AUGMENTED FIFTH CHORDS (AUG. or +)

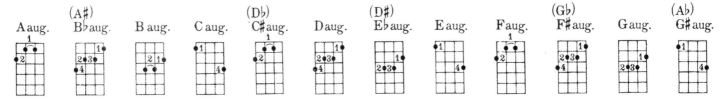

DIMINISHED SEVENTH CHORDS (Dim.)

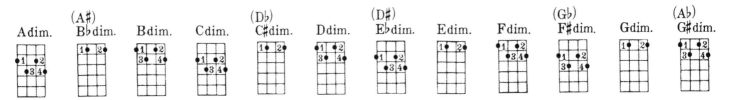

PRINCIPAL CHORDS IN MAJOR AND MINOR KEYS

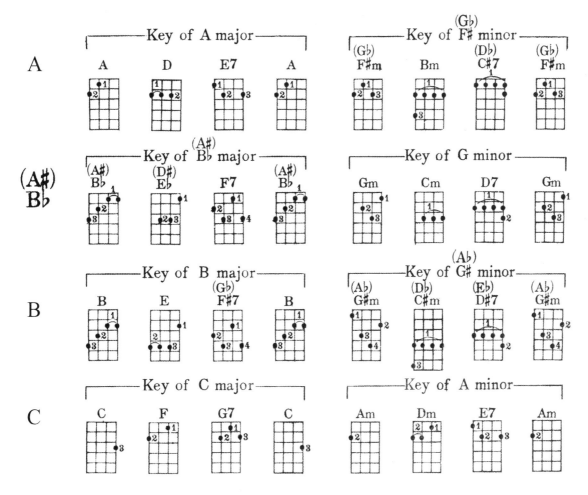

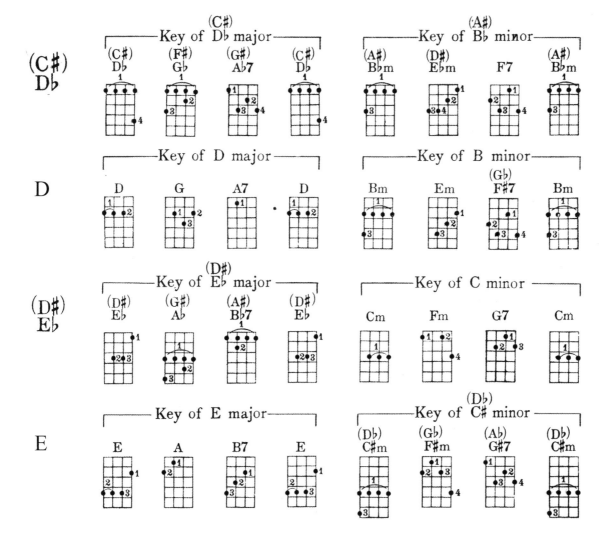

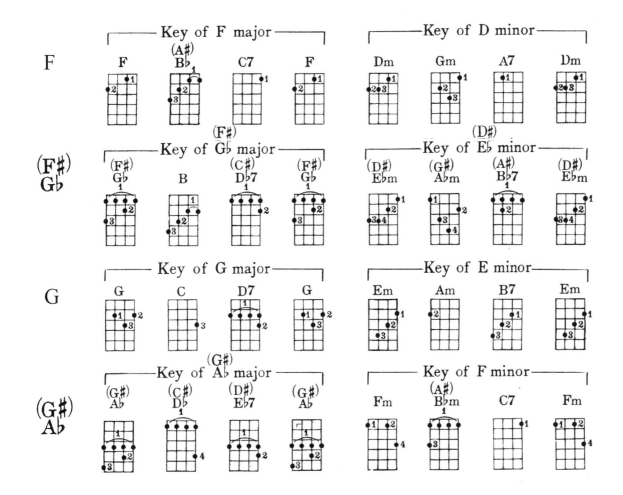

MAJOR CHORDS

Positions for

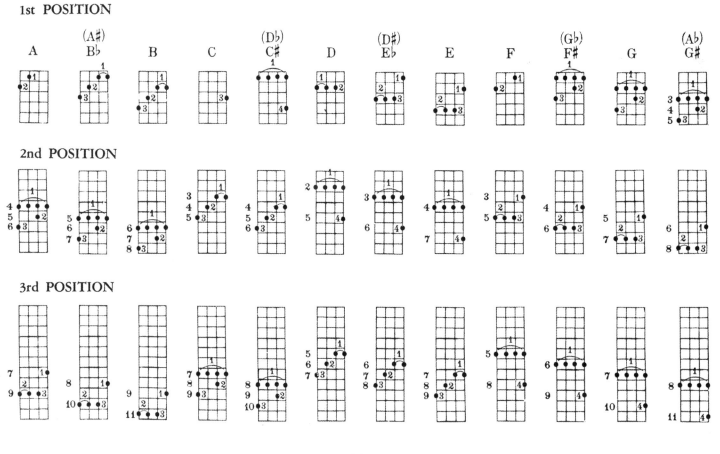

Positions for
MINOR CHORDS

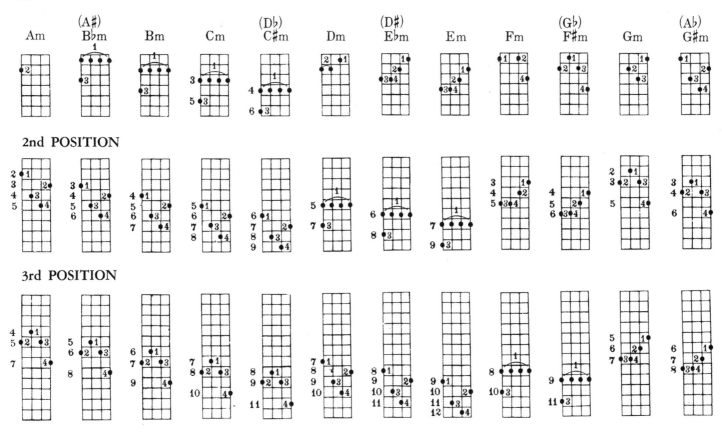

Positions for
DOMINANT SEVENTH CHORDS

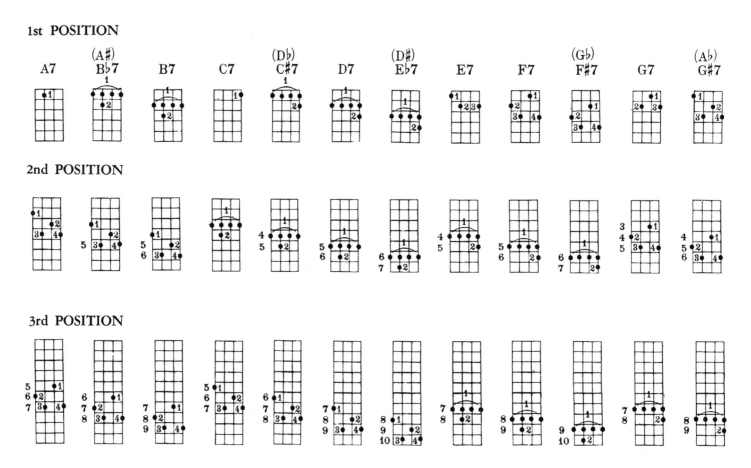

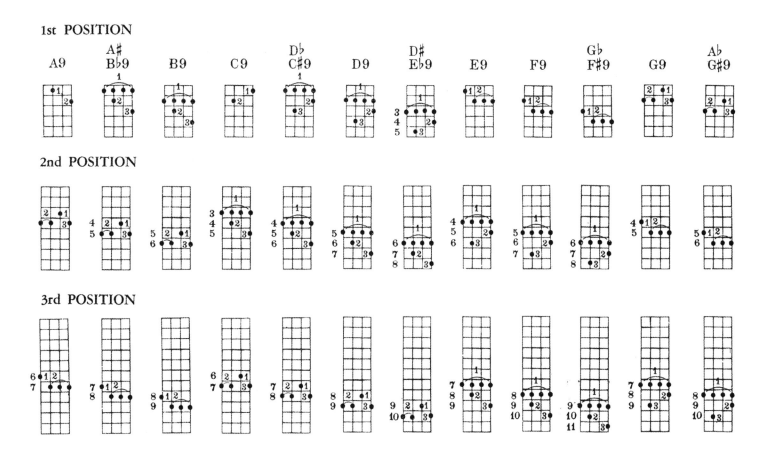

MINOR SEVENTH CHORDS

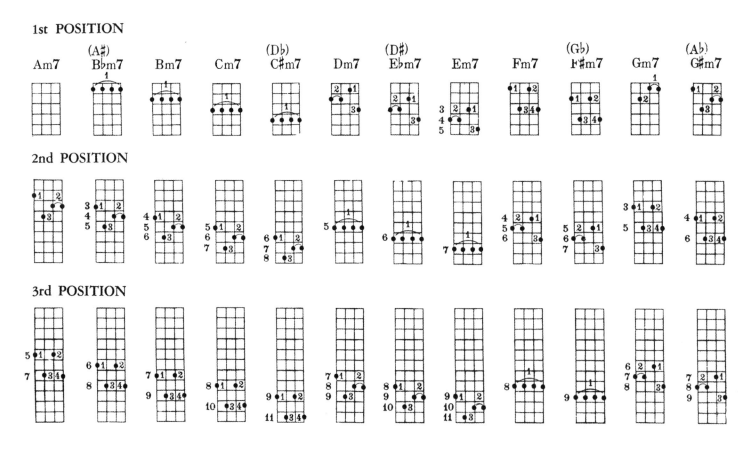

Positions for
MAJOR SIXTH CHORDS

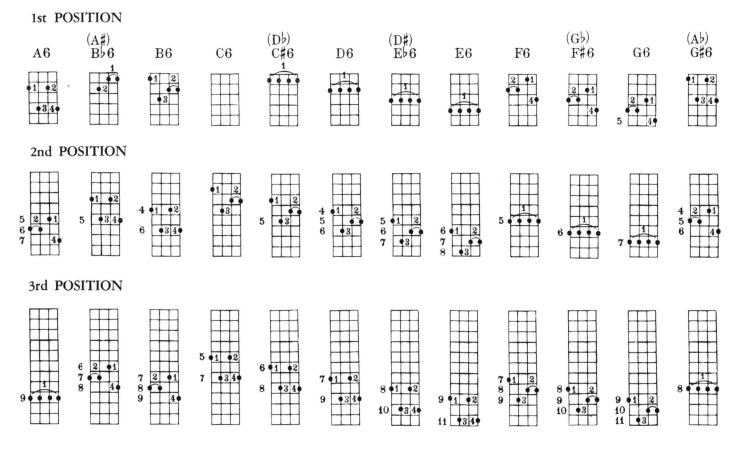

19

MINOR SIXTH CHORDS

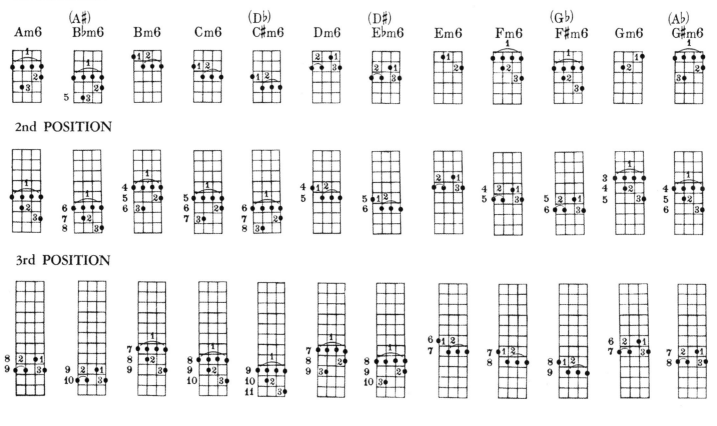

MAJOR SEVENTH CHORDS

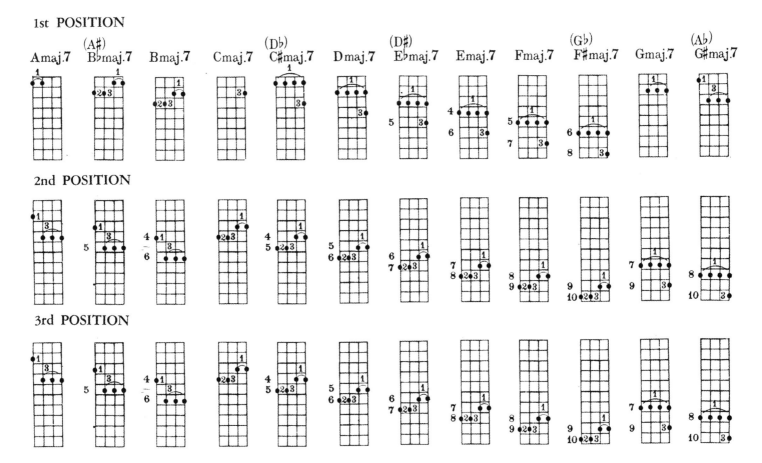

DOMINANT SEVENTH CHORDS WITH RAISED FIFTH (7th +5)

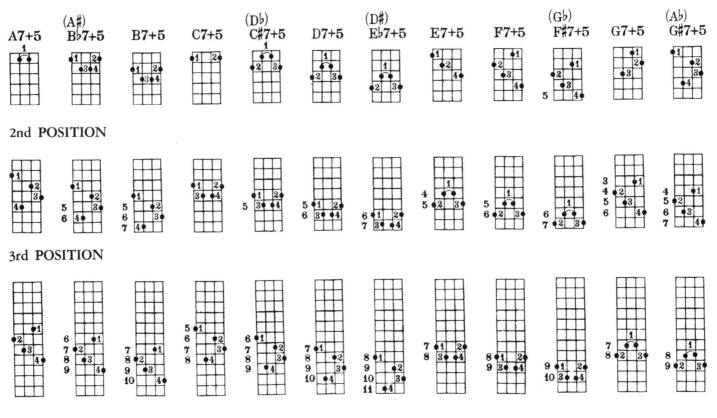

DOMINANT SEVENTH CHORDS WITH LOWERED FIFTH (7th – 5)

1st POSITION

A7-5   (A#) B♭7-5   B7-5   C7-5   (D♭) C#7-5   D7-5   (D#) E♭7-5   E7-5   F7-5   (G♭) F#7-5   G7-5   (A♭) G#7-5

2nd POSITION

3rd POSITION

AUGMENTED CHORDS

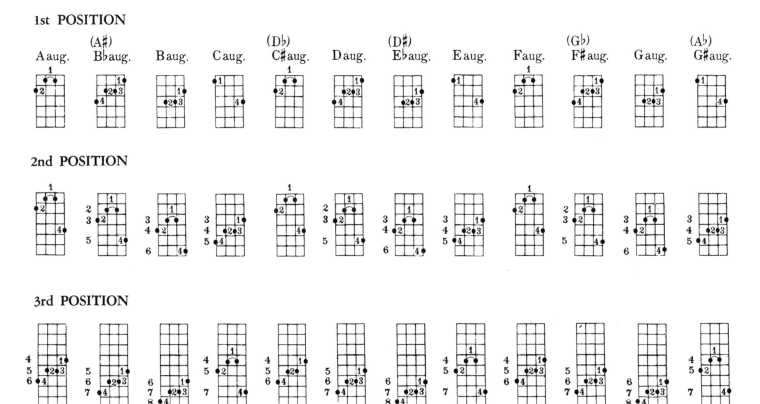

DIMINISHED SEVENTH CHORDS

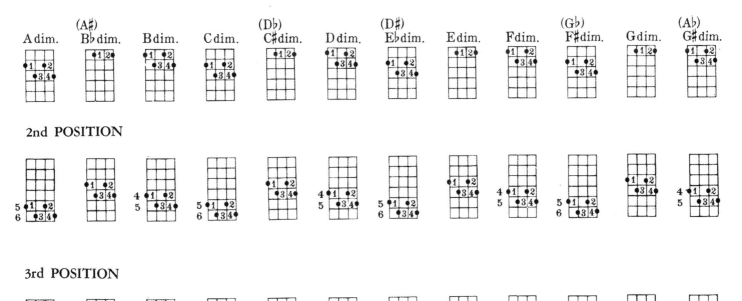

MODULATIONS

Modulations are great for intros or ending of songs

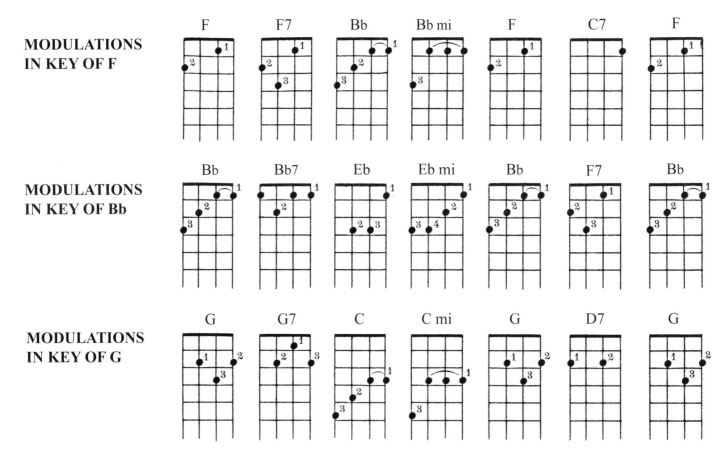

MODULATIONS

MODULATIONS IN KEY OF D

MODULATIONS IN KEY OF C

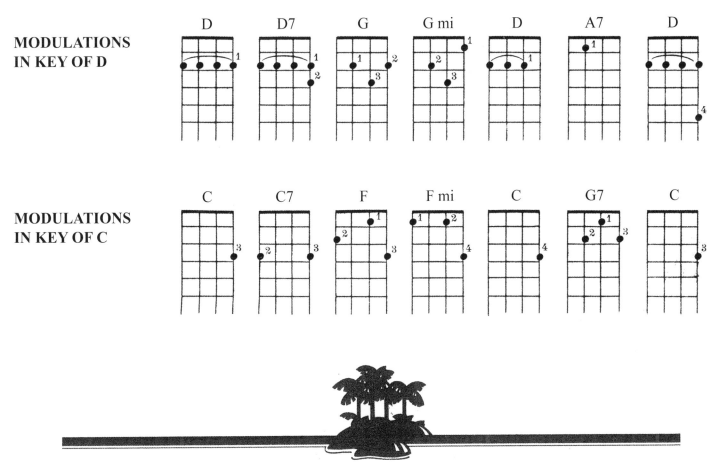

27

NOTE STUDY

On the "G" or 4th String

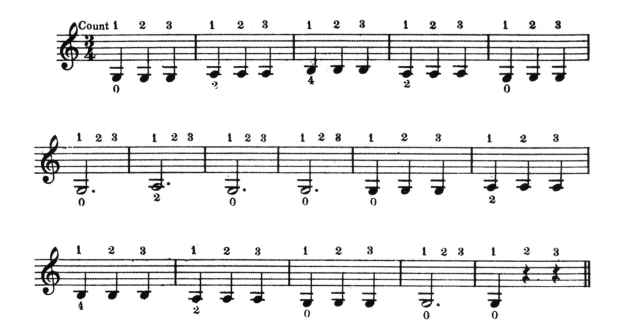

NOTE: Numbers below the notes show which Fret is to be pressed down.

On the "C" or 3rd String

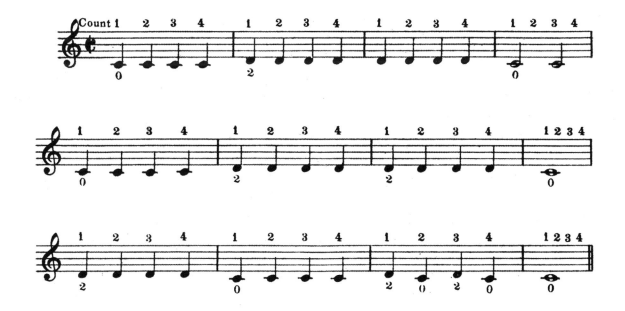

NOTE: Numbers below the notes show which Fret is to be pressed down.

On the "E" or 2nd String

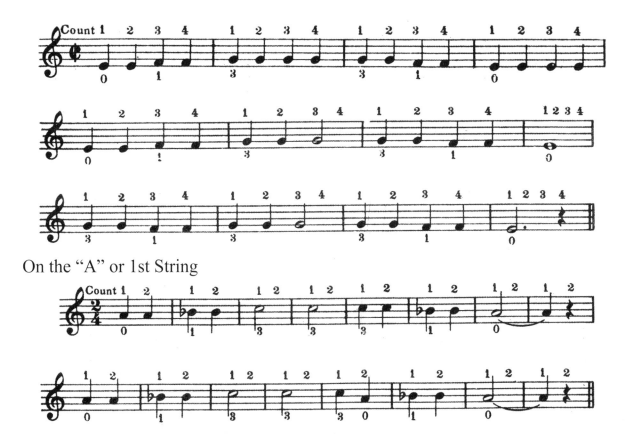

On the "A" or 1st String

SCALES ON ALL STRINGS

On the "G" or 4th String, G Scale

Music for the 4th string is written one octave lower than played.

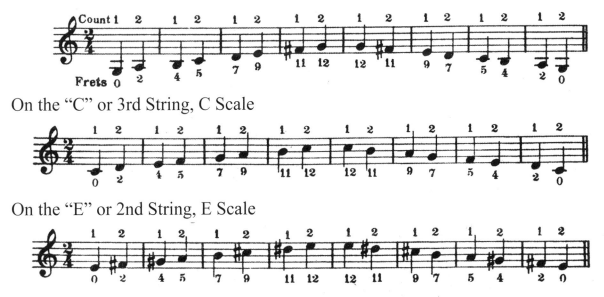

On the "C" or 3rd String, C Scale

On the "E" or 2nd String, E Scale

Pick the 3rd and 4th strings with thumb. Pick the 1st and 2nd strings with first finger.

On the "A" or 1st String, A Scale

31

More Great Ukulele Books from Centerstream...